Beautifully Broken

AF624615

Chelsea Whitlow

BookLeaf Publishing

Presentation by *BookLeaf Publishing*

Web: www.bookleafpub.com

E-mail: info@bookleafpub.com

ISBN: 9789357445030

First edition 2021

DEDICATION

To my family, my husband, and our soon-to-be-born baby boy. I am thankful for all of you, every time I've needed strength, you've been there to lift me up. I love all of you deeply and your support has made this possible.

ACKNOWLEDGEMENT

This book is written in remembrance of my past, although riddled with unsavory memories and abuse, my past is also full of laughter, big accomplishments, and a whole lot of love. I am thankful for that past and the struggles, because each memory has made me into me.

I am also thankful for BookLeaf Publishing and the opportunity to publish my very first book.

PREFACE

From falling in love, finding safety, and to beating a bad situation. Here's a toast to your past, but now it is over and you have to heal. Always remember that you are your best asset and no one can take away your resilience.

Embers

Like the embers left after a fire burns out,
My love for you is a breath away.
With some care, it can be lit again.
I will choose you each day.
Fire burning bright is beautiful until it turns to smoke.
Your eyes dancing with memories and mischief.
I'll never forget the words that were never spoken.
I wish loving you did not leave me broken.

Stones

Wrap me in you, build me, make me new
Hold onto me, hard and tight.
Love me and warm my cold bones at night.
Walk this path with me, in life and love.
Handle my heart softly, like a velvet glove.
Listening to water trickle over stones...
We hike this path together, never alone.

Emptied

Love was never the problem,
I have more than enough in my ever-repairing heart.
The problem was reciprocation.
I emptied from myself to have someone consistently starving for more.
You gorged yourself on everything that I gave,
While never refilling the bone dry challis.
That is why it was not enough for us.
Why love didn't fail, it failed to reach us both.

Unmoving

She has been beaten, broken, and shattered.
But, picked it all up and reassembled the jagged pieces.
Be fearful to try and knock her down again.
She is unmoving, and shifting her stance with the wind.
With but a smile, all you have left is your self-inflicted pain.

Unpinned

Don't you dare...
Ask me to dull my shine to make you seem brighter.
Don't you pretend...
To sympathize and break me all over again.
I used to believe all that you said was real,
No more-
Your hypnotizing narcissism will fail this time.
Today I unpin each layer of which you tried to stake down.
I slosh away my pain to embrace my strength.

Lesson Learned

I have learned a few things from you-
Piling lies on lies does not create truth.
Sweeping dirt under the rug will not make it clean.
What someone shows is not always what it seems.
You have buried yourself under a facade, too hard to dig out.
Karma has no mercy now, and now all around you show their doubt.
Now that you've been unmasked for the evil that you are.
There is no talking out of this one, your sweet words have now gone sour.

Choke

After all this time, people take what they want
from you.
Upon confrontation, they gaslight and say it is
not true.
Your burn those bridges and try to move on,
But it seems like each corner that you turn is so
wrong.
I was the blessing that your boorish hands
mishandled,
slipping through your fingers like a phantom.
Now that I've moved on, built new walls, you
think you'll break through.
But that will never happen, I hope when you say
my name it chokes you.

Love You More

I don't love you like yesterday,
Today I love you more.
Holding me up when I'm falling,
Never letting me hit the floor.
I want to wrap my arms around you, and hold you forever.
I have never tied lines so tight, and with you I'll never sever.
I love you more each day that you choose me.
Loving you has changed my world, and for once, I'm finally free.

Bow Out

I cannot do this anymore.
Lost sleep and rubbish lying on the floor.
I know that I'm better than this, above all this self blame.
Leaving was the best decision that I've made, but it hurts all the same.
I've questioned how I feel, what drew me in.
There is so much negative, where did the good begin.
I constantly blame myself, watching the curtains close on us.
Indiscretion completed together, only one taking the backlash is unjust.
I was responsible and strong, I don't know how.
I fell hardest but now I have to take a bow.

Not Love

I fooled myself into thinking that I was in love.
You spun all of these beautiful promises, but
then shattered my solid ground.
You took every ounce of my sweetness, stomped
on everything we dreamed up.
You turned the other cheek when I was down.
Now that you can't paint a pretty picture
anymore, you are left regretting.
Unfortunately for you, I've moved on and about
you, I'm forgetting.

Vines

Like vines twisting, changes happen at all
stages, throughout time.
Nothing worthwhile happens overnight.
In order to reach the stars, you have to see their
light.
Some experiences scar more and recovery is a
lot harder.
As long as movement continues forward, you
learn from it all and end up smarter.

Bird

Sitting quietly, a faint and desperate chirping
was heard.
Attention snatched, outside on the windowsill
was a small bird.
Withering in the elements, no will to fight.
You decided it needed you and took it in for the
night.
Every moment nourishing it, in spite of yourself.
Only worrying about the little bird above all
else.
Again the bird took flight because of your
kindness.
You are a healer, life-giver to the lifeless.
Remember that when times are hardest.
You saved that bird, and you are strong enough
to heal yourself as promised.

Starved

Sustained with my own affection.
Drowning in the glow of gaslights, barely
recognizing my own reflection.
Skin stretched over bones so tight.
You left me starved on memories, my sadness
protruding.
Ghostly white and living off of batteries, I want
to pull through.
How is one to forgive, when they still hate you?

Rain

Recalling that day, peeling my body off of the
bathroom floor.
Trying to form words, wondering if it is worth it
anymore.
I fell down, so hard and fast.
Longing to feel, but nothing seemed to last.
When I got out I finally tasted the rain.
Instead of the salt, like years, it was refreshing.
It was only a bad day and not a bad life.
I can do this, I will do this, no more regressing.

Candle

And then she felt it, a flicker deep inside.
Hope that she thought was lost, a flame she thought had died.
A glimmer of purpose and strength beginning.
When struggles wore her to bones, she now found herself swimming.
Where the air flitted between layers, while in the darkness she found a candle.
Perseverance and bravery, she used her fear as an example.

Name

Go ahead, backpedal, it's all you ever do.
Sinking money and time into things that cannot save you.
Funny, there is no question about the disfigured monster under your facade.
Thinking you've got us fooled, an image like a god.
You are at a standstill and throwing stones at bricks.
All have started wising up and won't fall for your old tricks.
It is simply dumb luck that our relatives are the same.
Unfortunately I can't say I don't know you, we share the same last name.

Irrelevant

I want to hate you,
Take all of this frustration and aim it.
Walk around like nothing is wrong,
Paint a lie a frame it.
Your stories and the truth are so different.
The only ones that flock to you are pathetic.
You have been diagnosed with Napoleon
Syndrome and your attempts are belligerent.
Even your family has to force themselves to be
sympathetic.
Walking on eggshells for fear of PTSD could
take a final toll.
Everything is fallacy, done for attention.
Demons like you have no soul.
It is time to realize, you aren't worth a mention.

Feather

But will you love her in the morning, when
daylight sees her skin?
Once her walls have been bulldozed and you felt
her fear from within.
Will you still think she's beautiful with tears in
her eyes?
Lips chapped and bleeding, she uncovered all
your lies.
She isn't a swipe right, but a memory for forever.
Remember when you walk away, you've taken a
piece of her forever.

www.ingramcontent.com/pod-product-compliance
Lightning Source LLC
Chambersburg PA
CBHW051721130826
49812CB00034B/1284
9789357445030